Women, Know Thyself: The most important knowledge is self-knowledge

By John G. Agno and Barbara A. McEwen

Copyright 2012

ISBN: 9780983586586

Readers should be aware that Internet websites offered as citations and/or sources for further information or book purchase may change or disappear between the time of writing and when read.

sales representatives or written sales materials. The advice and strategies contained herein may not be suitable for your situation. You should consult with a professional where appropriate. The authors shall be not be held liable for any loss of profit or any other personal or commercial damages, including but not limited to special, incidental, consequential, or other damages.

Table of Contents

Forward

Year after year, the authors have heard working women's frustrations and have helped them deal with massive internal conflicts.

Men with little insight into—or appreciation for—a woman's unique predicaments, biology, and socialization patterns have suggested how she "fix" her problem. However, their suggestions are based on what works for men—and those suggestions are largely unhelpful for women.

Long-standing cultural norms are hard to shake—
and women have a long list of those norms (many
of which are outdated and/or irrelevant) to
struggle against. One of these outdated norms
assumes that women should take care of others
while men take charge. Today's women want to
believe this is no longer the case. That is until they
run into the subtleties at play and come to realize
these expectations haven't changed significantly
over the years, despite the feminine "revolution"
that began in the 1970s.

Not only does our culture have concrete
expectations for women, women have expectations
of their own. A woman who has achieved
significant distinction in the workplace is still
expected to come home and fit into an age-old
stereotypical role of wife, mother, homemaker,
interior designer, cook, cleaner, entertainer,
educator, finance manager, shopper, gardener,
friend, daughter, granddaughter, sister, and
neighbor, volunteer. The list alone takes our
breath away!

Then women try to fill their roles outside the home. Their workplace piles on more expectations about a woman's role and her appropriate behavior. A woman brave enough, daring enough, or tired enough to step outside those boundaries often finds her involved in some form of guilt and internal or external conflict.

Is it any wonder that the self-help books currently available don't work well in relieving the pressures working women routinely face?

In examining this dilemma with a succession of clients, it was evident that women do not automatically experience the same professional issues that men routinely face. Instead, they struggle to be all things to all people— and along the way they neglect themselves and their own priorities.

Women have taken on tasks and then asked themselves why. We need to understand that there is a huge difference between being busy and doing the things that will help us achieve our goals or calling. It is amazingly easy to be blindsided by the things that matter least when what we want to be focusing on are those things that matter most. If we really don't care where we are going, then any road will get us there.

But, if we have a destination in mind, we need a good compass or GPS system—and even then, it is easy to get off track. This is where we must rely upon our inner compass. This book is intended to help you understand and work with your unique inner compass.

Understanding who we are, how other people see us and knowing what is important to us is critical to our success. As you learn more about yourself, you will know best how to manage your time and life in a way that gives you peace, a sense of fulfillment and the strength to handle the challenges ahead.

Self-awareness facilitates change.

Being unaware, we unconsciously engage our default behavior. Only when we become aware of something, are we able to make choices as to the action we wish to take.

Sometimes, just being aware, allows the problem to solve us--rather than requiring us to solve the problem.

We really don't know how the world works. We only perceive how the world works and our unique perception is based upon who we are and what we are aware of that is happening around us.

Here is a mental model to consider using in your world:

Beliefs influence perception.

Perception structures reality.

Reality suggests possibilities.

Possibilities generate choices.

Choices initiate actions.

Actions affect outcomes.

Outcomes impact beliefs.

<u>Awareness</u> facilitates change.

You will discover a new-found freedom, energy and sense of self as you make the changes in your life suggested in this book.

For a complete explanation of the insights within this book, you are encouraged to purchase, "**When Doing It All Won't Do: A Self-Coaching Guide for Career Women**" by John Agno and Barbara McEwen.

Both books are dedicated to all those hard working women who are willing to embrace liberating change.

Introduction

Most of us try to live our lives with far too little information about how life really works.

If you think about it, everything in life… from kitchen gadgets to the tools we use, come with very detailed instructions. Pages of them. But the thing that matters most to us, life itself, comes with no instructions. We have to discover it ourselves!

Our personalities are shaped by genetics and life experiences. In childhood, we decide what's important to us and that influences a great deal of our personality. And, we continuously evolve. Each of us is defined by many things – our emotional habits, our belief systems, our pattern of thoughts, our cultural upbringing, our preferences, our motivations, our style of relating to others, to name a few.

Some characteristics we share in common, some we don't. What we need to function well will often be quite different from what someone else will need. This is where self-knowledge and personal insight comes in. There is a big advantage in knowing ourselves and the type of environment in which we feel nurtured. But there is also a huge advantage in knowing how a partner, a child, or a co-worker thinks, feels and sorts information. Once we recognize that not everyone is like me and that each of us sees the world through their own lens, we will quickly realize that individuals will approach similar situations differently. It is not necessary that they do it just like me.

You cannot afford to miss the richness that comes with understanding your own personality and the benefit it brings to relationships. Take time to explore one or two <u>personality assessments</u>, with or without a coach.

It has been said that foresight is better than hindsight but we believe insight tops them all. <u>Learn your unique signature talents</u> and understand how when they are overused can become a weakness. Understand <u>how you stand out from others</u>.

As the world moves faster, when you are expected to do more with less, when teamwork and innovation are essential, when there are greater cultural and international concerns, understanding psychological types offers an unmatched resource.

Self-Understanding

"I want, by understanding myself, to understand others. I want to be all that I am capable of becoming." Katherine Mansfield

Let's face it: you are the most interesting and important subject in the entire world. You will always be at or near the center of your world. It's a comfortable place to be! So, one of the most exciting—and, often, one of the most intimidating—experiences lies in gaining a fuller understanding of just who you are.

Life is a perpetual process of becoming. To truly understand ourselves, we need to understand how we view ourselves, how others view us, and how we truly interact with others, not how we think we interact. Self-understanding means knowing what we need and how we desire to grow. It starts with two simple questions:

Do I like who I am?

Am I happy with the person I am becoming?

To answer honestly, we need to have crystal-clear insight into the person who bears our name and Social Security number.

We consciously as well as unconsciously create our own reality through our thoughts (what we tell ourselves), our emotions (how we feel), and our behaviors (how we act). If we are to become self-aware, we must be able to understand our thoughts, emotions, and behavior. Our ability to live the life we desire will depend on our level of self awareness, the thoughts we think, the choices we make, and the behavior we display.

Sociologists tell us that human beings see two ways: First, with our eyesight; secondly, with our minds (this is called insight). We know what we see in the mirror. Insight is a little more challenging.

Insight takes into consideration what makes us unique. If we are truly courageous, we will do a little research and take a good look at how our attitudes and actions are perceived by others.

Remember, attitude is always reflected in our behavior toward others. We won't be remembered by others for our determination or our dedication. We will be remembered by the way we made other people feel about themselves.

Since our entire lives are controlled by our attitudes, we must recognize the fact that our perceptions are involved in everything we think and do. A person cannot think negatively about another person and then feel good about their relationship. So, if we want successful relationships and successful lives, it is our responsibility to control what goes on in our minds. We need to monitor our "mind chatter" and alter our internal storytelling when it's necessary. Napoleon Hill was right when he said, "Keep your mind on the things you want and off the things you don't want."

Self-awareness requires us to recognize our personal energy fluctuations because they determine how we respond physically and mentally. Some of us tend to get shrill and whine when we're tired. Others shut down and withdraw into silence. We each have different patterns, so we each need to recognize our own individual responses. Although subtle, managing our energy peaks and lows is a creative way to become more effective. Others will know if we face a situation that is difficult or irritating, and they will reward or condemn us for our response. For instance:

One writer we know took her daughter to the mall at the end of a very long and frustrating day. The clerks were struggling to fix the cash machine and the check-out line grew longer and longer, the clock seemed to tick faster and faster, and our friend's patience grew very thin. When she finally reached the counter, only to discover the machine had broken down once again, she opened her mouth to say something withering. Fortunately, before she had a chance to unload her frustration, the clerk asked her if she was an author. She looked surprised and nodded.

"You were so nice—you signed six of your books for my kids," the clerk said, smiling. "They love your books."

Our friend smiled back and left the store vowing never to get irritable or short-tempered in public again. "You never know where you'll meet someone who will recognize you," she pointed out when she confessed that story. "I'm fifty years old and I'm still learning valuable lessons about life."

It's important to remind ourselves that we will be judged, for good or ill, based on our behavior. One simple way to make things easier for us is to plan our schedule so we interact with others when we are at our peak in energy—our writer friend probably should have scheduled a shopping trip with her daughter on another day.

Therein is one important secret to maintaining successful relationships: energy management.

Energy management means playing to our strengths, recognizing when we're capable of doing our best, and using those times productively. We need to learn and abide by a vital lesson: Don't allow unimportant activities to swallow up our best working hours—we need to budget them, allocate them, and dedicate them for the important things.

Most of us spend our high-energy times dealing with the things that might be urgent, but may not be important. We finish the easy things on our "To Do" list because it feels good to cross off a long line of items. But the things we're crossing off may not be the things that will help us achieve our goals. We need to keep those goals in mind constantly. When we allow interruptions during our peak times and when we procrastinate—leaving the big jobs until we are under a time crunch—we are showing the classic

signs of poor time management. And when that happens, it's almost guaranteed that unexpected events will pop up and wreak havoc with our schedule and our stress levels.

Many of us have suffered from a chronic case of under-planning and over-scheduling at one time or another.

Some of us are experts at it! Despite our optimism and experience, "To Do" list items almost always take longer to complete than we anticipate. So, if we wait too long to tackle the important jobs, we find ourselves burning the midnight oil, neglecting a pleasurable activity we'd been anticipating, or losing time with a friend or family member. And then we wonder why we feel stressed!

The solution is simple. We need to study our peak performance periods and make the best use of them.

These blocks of time need to be set aside for our biggest and most important tasks. This is the time when we feel energetic and refreshed, most capable of focusing on those things that are most important or require our undivided attention. Most of us will have at least two of these peak periods during the day. Many of us know if we're morning people or night people, but sometimes we don't stop to identify our two (or three!) most productive high-energy times.

We also need to identify our low-performance or less-than-peak- performance periods. These are the blocks of time when we plan to do activities that don't require much focus or energy such as answering emails, returning phone calls, scheduling routine meetings, talking about staff issues, etc.

In order to perform at our best, we all need to re-energize and re-charge our batteries on a regular basis, not just during vacations and national holidays. Many people use early mornings, late afternoons, or early evenings to catch their breath, take a break, meditate, pray, think, or otherwise plan. These are also ideal times to spend with the family, reading, listening to music, watching TV, or enjoying exercise or a hobby.

Travel days offer golden opportunities to re-energize. Don't waste the hours waiting in an airport lobby or riding in a vehicle. Use those times to think, plan, jot down ideas, read a good book, or catch up with someone or something. When we do, we find ourselves feeling prepared, fit, and rested for the meeting or event that arrives at the end of the trip. Often we can do our best creative thinking when we capture "loose" time and tame it.

Explore Your Signature Talents

"To be what we are, and to become what we are capable of becoming, is the only end of life."

Baruch Spinoza

We all have talents and skills. The question is: What are we doing with them?

Sociologists report that more than ever before, human beings are thinking about the significance of their lives, searching for ways to pursue a meaningful purpose. This genuine spiritual concern involves traditional views of religion, but it is even broader, encompassing the entire human condition. In our heart of hearts, we all yearn to utilize our talents and make a difference in the world.

Each of us has what we call core signature talents that set us apart from others. We also have signature themes, which are reflected in what we like and find easy to do. For instance, one person may be skilled at math but doesn't enjoy doing more than balancing her checkbook. Instead, she loves the creative process involved in making quilts, planning sales materials, and decorating spaces. Although math is a talent, it isn't a theme in her life. She has other themes that are imbedded in her heart.

The best advice we can give you is to identify, understand, celebrate, and, most importantly, use your signature talents in as many ways as you can, as creatively as you can. If you need confirmation about your special talents and the themes of your life, ask the people who know you best. Listen carefully and consider what they say. Pay attention. Their remarks may be road signs directing you to different paths, to journeys you might otherwise never consider. When we tune in to our talents, we can create a vision for our lives, and we will find that this will heighten our passion, help us select the right career, and give us confidence to reach our goals.

When we feel directionless, without a sense of what we are "called" to do, life becomes confusing, worrying, and frustrating. If we ignore our options, we feel as if we are spinning our wheels, and we miss the satisfaction that comes with a job well done, a job that we enjoy passionately. We worry that if we decide to change, we may be making another poor choice. Then depression often sets in, and people complain of feeling tired and useless. Energy fizzles when we are unmotivated and our actions appear to be ineffectual.

When we feel pushed in various directions by our circumstances, we become reactors instead of co-creators in our own lives. What we don't feel is any control of our lives.

We all know people who question their career choice, or lack of one. (Or we may have done it ourselves at one time or another.) That happens when we are frustrated because we feel underutilized or when we are doing tasks that "don't fit" our expertise or interests. People who are consistently discontent with what they are doing with their lives will find that they are not using their signature talents in a satisfactory way. This has occurred for one of two reasons: either because they are unsure of what their specific signature talents are or because they are in a position where their talents are not being used.

Work-related frustrations can happen at any time in our lives, but particularly when we've been in an unvarying position for a while. Mid-life crises are very common; these are times when people wonder "Is this all there is to life?" or "How did I ever get in this position?" We can avoid or at least lessen mid-life crises if we start the self-exploration process as early as possible. We should regard the process as illuminating and exciting rather than painful. Identifying and utilizing our signature talents can make the difference between a life well lived and a life fraught with anxiety and depression.

Three excellent books that focus on the importance of knowing and developing signature themes or talents are "*Strengths Finder 2.0*" by Tom Rath, "*Now, Discover Your Strengths*" by Marcus Buckingham and Donald O. Clifton, and "*StandOut*" by Marcus Buckingham. These books provide the reader with a unique code that can be used to take an online self-assessment to learn his or her top signature talents. Your enduring and unique signature talents are ranked by each of these self-assessments and provide you with unique insight in a comprehensive report.

Since many of us feel as though we are wandering through life plagued by the nagging suspicion that we are inventing our lives as we go along, we are fearful of asking ourselves how to best live our life. And this fear confines us. Unsure of the person we really are, we define ourselves by our knowledge or our achievements. And, when this is the case, we become reluctant to change careers or learn new ways of doing things because we might be required to redefine our identity.

Furthermore, because we are unsure of the person we might discover under our own skin, we don't bother to investigate the identity of anyone else— after all, how can we know another if we don't know ourselves? Instead, we resort to defining people by their education, ethnicity, gender, sexual identity, religion, profession, or other superficial markers.

But, we can avoid all these fears and uncertainties by figuring out who we are. Only then will we be confident enough to go off exploring. In order to figure out who we are, we must identify our top signature themes. These signature themes will unerringly draw the picture of who we are, and they will convince us that we are not making up our lives as we go along, that our achievements and successes are not accidental.

Our signature themes influence every single choice we make. They explain our successes and achievements.

This kind of self-awareness leads to a strong sense of self-confidence. No longer will the question "Are you living your life?" intimidate us. We will know that no matter what our choice of profession, no matter what trajectory our career has taken, no matter where we live, if we are applying, refining, and polishing our top signature themes, then we are indeed living the life we were intended to live.

Our signature themes will point us to True North. For example, Author John G. Agno's top signature talents in the *StrengthsFinder* are Individualization, Maximizer, Strategic, Relator, and Activator and in the *StandOut* are Equalizer and Pioneer.

The answers to many questions related to a career path is "Play to your strengths" and "Follow your heart."

That isn't as hard as it sounds.

Throughout our lives, we all need to continue to refine and develop our natural talents, building them into our signature strengths. It would be a tragedy to overlook these abilities, just because they come easily. One of the best things we can do for ourselves is to take the time to consider and discover our individual talents—and then apply them. These talents are not only priceless and precious, but also vital to our success. Identifying and classifying our strengths will answer a lot of questions about who we are and why we respond the way we do. They are also the key to job satisfaction and our ability to achieve our goals. The more opportunities we have to use our talents, the happier and more satisfied we will become.

That said, we can't waste any more time! We need to align our lives with our signature talents!

You'll find that exploring your special gifts and then applying them will generate the passion that comes from a commitment to goals specific and unique to you. Once you know more about your talents, it is far easier to determine what it is you are meant to do. You'll find that your new-found energy and enthusiasm will drive you forward to exciting and challenging adventures in your work life as well as in your personal life.

Discovering Your Signature Talents

There are a number of ways to identify our signature talents, but let's start with a journey down "Memory Lane."

Go back in time and trace when and where you've felt fulfilled, happy, and accomplished. List the talents you associate with that success. This is not the time for modesty. On this page, you are invited—actually, you are required—to blow your own horn. Celebrate your successes at all stages of your life, and identify what talents and skills were at their base. Feel free to add more lines—or even pages—to this worksheet if you need them.

My talents:

Occasionally, this process will bring even greater surprises. One of the youngest female partners in a Big Five consulting firm had decided to take a general management position in an industrial company to further her career. Unfortunately, the job didn't align with her signature talents and she became very uncomfortable about her career path. Through self-assessments and personal coaching, she realized that her results-oriented personality was much more in tune with consulting projects than in a caretaking management role. She decided to return to the path where she had been most comfortable and successful. She now leads teams of consultants.

Still Unsure?

To complete your list, ask friends, family members, former employers and employees, and associates to give you feedback. Then check out on-line resources. Here are a few that will offer valuable help—and a fun and intriguing experience:

http://www.StrengthsFinder.com

http://www.SelfAssessmentCenter.com

http://www.StandOut.tmbc.com

http://www.AuthenticHappiness.org

http://www.HappinessHypothesis.com

Occasionally, our signature talents are so strong that they need to be moderated.

Jennifer, a public relations executive, offers an example. Her two top signature talents were identified as being very positive and very adaptable. The problem she faced was her tendency to take on far too many projects because she was so positive and adaptable. As her stress mounted and deadlines loomed, she called into play her third signature talent, restoration, in a desperate attempt to resuscitate and rekindle failing projects. Working with an executive coach, she learned that overextending her top talents interfered with her ability to do her work well. She adjusted her behavior to become more selective in accepting new projects.

The lesson? Use your talents wisely and in balance!

Put Your Signature Talents to Work

Look at each talent individually and consider how and when you've applied it successfully. Then brainstorm about occasions when you can pull that talent out of your tool kit and put it to work for you and those around you.

Our advice is to leverage your talents. When problems and challenges arise, mentally refer to your talent list and select which ones you can put into play to help solve the problem. Take time to think that question through—it will save you countless hours and provide you with immense satisfaction.

When you apply your strengths to the areas and issues that are important in your life, you will automatically adjust your focus toward positive outcomes, not negative ones.

Knowing who you are and what you do best—and then applying that knowledge—will propel you forward faster than you would think possible.

Begin by reflecting on your innate signature talents. As you build and develop these talents you will experience a new-found sense of well-being, peace, and satisfaction.

Do What You Do Best

"Nature arms each person with some faculty which enables us to do easily some feat impossible to any other." Ralph Waldo Emerson

At one time or another, all of us have dreamed of becoming a heroine, a celebrity, a VIP, or someone else who stands out above the crowd. We know we have talent but we often resist taking a chance or going after our dream. Sometimes life seems like a runaway train that we are scrambling to catch.

We have to discover the way we want to live our lives for ourselves!

The first part of the discovery process is to learn about who we are. We need to become the Lewis and Clark of our own personal territory, discovering our strengths, weaknesses, triggers, motivations, tendencies, skills, goals, hopes, wishes, expectations, and themes. Early in our lives, we understand that we have a personality unique from everyone else's. Later we'll understand that personalities are shaped by our genetics, our personal life experiences, and the manner in which we interpret those experiences. Life is one long succession of learning experiences—and all too often we have to repeat the same lesson over and over again before we learn it by heart.

An old saying points out, if we don't learn the lessons that life sends our way, they will simply dress up in different clothes and march right back into our lives.

Starting in childhood, we begin to realize what is important to us. Those decisions will influence and create the person we become. Each of us is defined by many things, including our emotional habits, belief systems, pattern of thoughts, cultural upbringing, references, motivations, spiritual beliefs, and our style of relating to others, to name a few. All those elements are part of the map we follow on our personal journeys to self-discovery.

We share some of our characteristics with those people closest to us, others we don't. Even identical twins vary in characteristics, talents, and themes. We each establish our own personal criteria in order to function well. This is where self-knowledge and personal insight become important.

Environments are crucial. Nurturing, healthy, safe environments allow us to soar without fears or worries. Those of us who are aware of the type of environment in which we feel both nurtured and challenged have a big advantage, because when we become independent we can create that environment for ourselves.

Knowing how a partner, a child, or a co-worker thinks, feels, and sorts information will help us help them become successful—and when that happens, we, too, will become successful because we have been a positive catalyst for their journey.

An important aspect of self-discovery occurs when we recognize that individuals are all unique, that each of us sees the world through our specific lens. This is the perspective from the inside looking out. We're not better or worse, we're just unique. When we accept that fact, we begin to understand the importance of allowing individuals to approach situations in their own way, both in personal and professional arenas.

Our partners, children, or colleagues don't need to handle things just like we do. In fact, it can be detrimental if they try. What a boring place the world would be if we all acted and thought alike!

The second part of the discovery process pulls us outside ourselves and into the experiences of others, which will enrich our lives incalculably. We can amass a great wealth in lifetime experiences by learning from others. We don't have to re-invent the wheel; we can learn from someone else and use our energies to discover other things. Make a point of learning everything you can about the people, activities, and things that matter most to you. There are many ways to do this.

Once you've started the process of self-discovery, look for input. Ask questions. Search for feedback. As Ken Blanchard, author and speaker would say, "Feedback is the breakfast of champions." Because some feedback can make us feel uncomfortable or sound as if we are seeking praise, too few of us purposefully seek constructive feedback—and yet feedback is an invaluable tool for improvement.

As we discover what it is we love to do and we begin to practice developing our skills, work will no longer feel like work. We will be anxious to continue improving, we will be enthusiastic about what each new day brings, we will have renewed energy, and we will become passionate about sharing our experiences.

However, knowing, reading, studying, and listening to others about what it is that we do best is not enough. We must be willing to take action.

What Do You Know?

Recognize those activities, places, and opportunities that naturally appeal to you. These are where your interests, talents and gifts reside. It is up to you to mine the gold that which lies within.

Start mining.

Manage Your Default Behavior

"Everyone thinks of changing the world, but few think of changing themselves." Leo Tolstoy

As people become more self-aware, they are usually amazed at the abilities of the conscious mind to choose, handle situations with deliberation, and behave appropriately for different occasions. On the flip side, the unconscious mind is a powerful force driving our behavior. Within our unconscious lie veiled assumptions and beliefs that formulate what is called default behavior. The dictionary defines default as the "failure to perform a task or fulfill an obligation," which means that default behaviors are reactive responses that occur when we fail to consider the appropriate response.

Becoming aware of our personal reactive tendencies is crucial if we want to make sense of our toxic behaviors, understand why we have permitted these gremlins to continue, and develop a plan for taming them.

Our attitudes are choices, some of the most important choices we will ever make. Attitudes are reflections of what goes on inside our heads. They affect everything we do—positively or negatively. A negative attitude acts like the accelerator of a car. When we put our pedal to the metal, we learn very quickly that driving can indeed be dangerous to our health and to our career aspirations. Default behaviors occur when we decide not to act, but to react. And default behaviors may not represent our best side or our ideal self.

Here is an example of default behavior:

Ebela had the reputation of a complainer. She will tell you that she can do anything better than anyone else: her direct reports, her colleagues, even her boss. That attitude breeds impatience, and Ebela is impatient and difficult to please because she sets her standards so high and nobody, she knows, is quite as capable, as committed, or as smart as she is.

Unfortunately, though, she is oblivious to the way her negative attitude and default behaviors (whining, complaining, and criticizing) had created a dysfunctional team.

After repeated efforts to curb her behavior, her boss let Ebela go, to everyone's relief. Her boss noted that the day Ebela left the workplace for the last time; a weight was lifted from the office, replaced with an atmosphere of camaraderie and positive energy.

The lesson? Each of us plays a significant part in the lives of everyone with whom we meet, work, live, and interact. In just one day, we have the power to influence a wide network of people positively or negatively.

Deciding how best to approach a situation:

Allows us to control impulses and select the most appropriate behaviors.

Shows us how to avoid reacting in negative and potentially self-limiting ways.

Makes us more understanding of others.

Reduces conflict, within ourselves and others.

Becoming aware of the effect our personality and default tendencies have on the people in our lives helps to engineer better communication and leadership styles. Effective leaders know that what people value deeply will move them most powerfully in their work. Because these leaders are aware of their own guiding principles, values, vision, assumptions and beliefs, they practice the art of not automatically defaulting to a behavior that is inappropriate for the situation. Instead, they focus on appropriate situational behaviors.

Unless we are conscious of our default behaviors, we will automatically return to them. We can make choices about our behaviors only when we are aware of them.

How many default tendencies exist?

Here is a preliminary list taken from a sampling of self-assessments:

The Enneagram is a dynamic personality system that describes nine distinct and fundamentally different patterns of thinking, feeling and acting. Each of the nine patterns is based on an explicit perceptual filter. This filter determines what you pay attention to, how you direct your energy and what you need in life for survival and satisfaction.

Enneagram, Type One (The Reformer or Perfectionist)

The Reformer, or Perfectionist, believes that she is responsible for critiquing, criticizing, suggesting, or improving everyone involved in a situation. Her default behavior ranges from being nosy to a conviction that her own opinion is better than everyone else's. She can be overly judgmental and she may lose control easily.

Enneagram, Type Eight (The Challenger or Protector)

The Challenger believes she is capable of taking on new challenges because she is charismatic and persuasive—and she knows best. Her default behaviors could range from "I'll do it myself" to applying pressure on others. She might display defiance and push others to their limits.

The DISC is based on a four-quadrant model that reliably describes four dimensions of human behavior (Dominance, Influence, Steadiness and Conscientiousness). Some people fall into one quadrant, others fall into two, and some may fall into three. There are 15 unique patterns that most commonly occur and are known as classical profile patterns.

DISC, Highly Conscientious

The Highly Conscientious woman believes that in-depth research and attention to even minute details are critical. She is rule-oriented rather than people-oriented, and her default behaviors could range from a great reluctance to make decisions (because she always wants more information), to becoming stubborn, tactless, or sarcastic.

DISC, Highly Dominant

This woman believes she is a calculated risk-taker. She is self-assured, smart, and competitive. She seldom listens to others, and can become blunt, forceful, even overly domineering.

The Myers-Briggs Type Indicator (MBTI) instrument is a four-quadrant model that was developed by Isabel Myers and Katharine Briggs as an application of Carl Jung's theory of psychological types. This theory suggests that we have opposite ways of gaining energy (extraversion or introversion), gathering or becoming aware of information (sensing or intuition), deciding or coming to a conclusion about certain information (thinking or feeling), and dealing with the world around us (judging or perceiving).

Myers–Briggs Type Indicator (MBTI), Feeling

Empathetic, compassionate, and accommodating, this woman can get annoyed at being taken advantage

of. She might try hard to avoid conflict, and she can become overly upset and emotional.

Myers–Briggs Type Indicator (MBTI), Extroversion

Believing in her own abilities, this woman always wants to contribute. Her default behaviors could range from excessive talking and poor listening skills to intolerance, interruptions, and rudeness.

Each of these characteristics has important strengths and commendable skills, but she needs to realize that an overused skill can become a weakness. For example, a woman who focuses on the future relies upon her insight, intuition, and conceptual skills. She is practically guaranteed to find the fact-finder boring.

She needs to understand that an over extension of her strengths in certain situations could be disastrous to her career and personal life. Focusing solely on the future and its potential, to the exclusion of regard for the present, can prove to be a weakness.

Emotional Intelligence (EI or EQ)

As much as 80% of adult 'success' can be attributed to emotional intelligence, according to Daniel Goleman, author of "*Emotional Intelligence*." He says that the difference between a good leader and an excellent leader is almost entirely based on her emotional intelligence ("EI" or "EQ" for Emotional Quotient).

The Center for Creative Leadership suggests that 75% of careers are derailed for reasons related to poorly developed EI competencies; including the inability to effectively resolve interpersonal conflicts, the inability to provide satisfactory team leadership, the inability to adapt to change, or the inability to elicit trust.

The woman capable of recognizing and acknowledging her default tendencies is a woman with a high level of emotional intelligence. She knows that poor behavior elicits negative emotions, and that negative emotions are destructive to relationships, personal and professional success, and her own self-esteem. She works hard to choose between her default behaviors and more appropriate responses.

When we work conscientiously to develop our emotional intelligence, we become sensitive not only to our own emotional needs, but also to what others need and require of us. How we handle our emotions and manage our relationships can determine our success in life.

Business leaders of today realize that EI is a competency that affects almost every aspect of our lives and everything we do. Our IQ is relatively fixed, but our EI can be improved significantly. Executive coaching can help clients improve in this area.

Let's Be Honest With Ourselves

Think about our own default behaviors. What behavioral tendencies do you exhibit under stress? (Raising your voice, becoming silent, interrupting others, stamping away from discussions, gossiping about others, etc.?)

What, if any, of the few sample personality types listed above might describe you?

Take the time to research your particular behavior type; as the more we know about ourselves, the more we can alter, fix, and fine-tune our behavior.

Make a Change: Where Needed

The key to successful personal relations lies in being constantly aware of two things:

You will want to embrace and develop your skills, but at the same time be aware that when they are overused, they can become a weakness.

Just because a woman can speak well in front of thousands, does not mean she should take center stage at all times. She might benefit from a commitment to developing listening skills, and encouraging others to speak up.

All of us have default behaviors that are often tied to our assumptions and beliefs. Being vigilant about when, where, and why these offensive behavioral tendencies surface will allow us to exert better control over our actions.

One way to learn about our default behaviors is to involve a close friend, partner, spouse, or family member in helping you to identify your "danger" signs. You might establish a signal between the two of you, to graciously indicate an opportunity to back off/cool down/shut off.

As with all change, we cannot simply think we will behave differently next time. To do so, we will need to visualize and practice new responses.

Learn How to Manage Stress

"Is everything as urgent as your stress would imply?" Carrie Latet

War. Terrorism. The economy. Crime rates. Declining standards in education. World hunger. Poverty. National elections. Rising costs. Depression. Job worries. The price tag for a college and graduate school education. Paying bills. Health issues. Weather-related disasters.

We live in stressful times. Television and radio shows bombard us with pictures and tales of disasters, natural and man-made. We no longer live small lives, we are members of a fragile global economy. So much of what stresses us—such as that list above—is beyond our control.

Coupled with this, we sometimes stagger under the weight of our personal burdens, everything from managing the home to maintaining relationships, handling workplace issues, addressing health concerns, finances, and day-to-day decisions.

Scientists have pointed out that moderate stress for women can actually help us perform at a higher level, but persistent stress can be debilitating and dangerous. Stress eats away at our ability to manage both our time and our responsibilities. Some wear their stress as a badge of honor to show how much they can handle. The underlying message is "Look at me. I'm Superwoman!" But that is not a healthy way to live.

Beware: Stress affects us both physically and psychologically. Physically, we might feel the proverbial butterflies in our stomachs, a pounding in our chest, or knots in our stomach during a stressful situation.

We can handle those for short periods of time, but if the situation continues, the negative physical and psychological affects will increase. When we are continually under chronic stress, our bodies react negatively sooner or later.

Each of us has a limit beyond which stress becomes toxic, even deadly. And everyone's limit is different, so we cannot predict what we can handle. Under prolonged stress, our resistance drops, our performance declines, our mental well-being gets derailed. There isn't a quick fix to eliminating stress, but successful people learn how to manage their stress.

Stress Reduction Takes Practice

The first step in stress reduction is to be able to identify stress-reduction activities that work well to help us manage our stress. Meditation, prayer, and exercise are proven winners for just about everyone, but there are other measures that can have great beneficial effects: reading, watching television, a walk in the woods, crafts, music, yoga, fishing, a coffee break out of the office, lunch with a friend, a visit with someone special, gardening, crafts. Just as you cannot read a fitness magazine and automatically become fit, you cannot read about stress reduction and have stress automatically dissipate. It takes practice to train our minds to focus on positive things.

In his book "*Life's Greatest Lessons*," Hal Urban talks about a faculty member, Tim Hansel, who had mastered the most powerful skill of all—the ability to affirm others. He tells us that affirm, in his opinion, is the most powerful word in our language. It means looking for and finding the good in people. It means building others up and encouraging them. It means finding reasons for praise and applause. It means nurturing and being supportive. It means reinforcing what others do well.

Stress is the reverse of affirming. It is negative. It tears others down. It lays blame. It is a belief that we need to change others or change a specific situation. We reduce stress only when we let go of our conviction that we can change others. When we take responsibility for ourselves alone and we allow others to be who they are, then we will find our stress levels drop significantly.

Too often we can't capture the feeling of contentment because of material worries, immaterial worries, or because of a sense of frustration about the good things we haven't made time for in our lives. Think about those for a moment, then consider what—if anything—you can do to make your dreams a reality.

You deserve that! If you can, get started on these—they will be sure ways to reduce or eliminate stress and to increase a sense not only of contentment, but excitement.

Hal Urban goes on to conclude that one of the most common mistakes we make is overlooking life's simple truths: There is a relationship between old-fashioned goodness and our health and well-being.

Here's to being kind and being healthy.

Identify Signs of Stress

We all move to the beat of a different drummer, as writer and naturalist Henry David Thoreau pointed out.

What is stressful for some of us is exciting and energizing for others. As we get to know ourselves better, we need to identify—and avoid—situations, people, and activities that are too stressful for us.

Consider the "under-the-skin" perspective, looking at the issue from the other person's point of view. Try to put yourself into that person's head and heart, considering what you know about her or him. What insights can you acquire?

Think about what everyone needs from you. Before making assumptions or expectations about the behavior of others, it is important to look at the situation objectively. Define the different points of view. For example,

The Situation:

Cathy and Jeff have solid careers, money in the bank, a lovely home, and two delightful daughters. Both have well-paying jobs, both enjoy travel, and both enjoy dining out. But Jeff consistently says no to Cathy's suggestions for vacations, weekend get-aways, or more expensive restaurant suggestions.

Cathy's Perspective:

We work hard and we deserve opportunities to relax and have fun. That would be good for us and good for our marriage. His fixation on money and savings drives me crazy!

Jeff's Perspective:

My parents never had money for anything—not even a home. We actually spent two years homeless, living in a car that Dad moved from one bad neighborhood to another. Neither of them could hold down a job because they were alcoholics. I don't want my family to suffer from a lack of money.

The Solution:

Cathy needed to understand Jeff's personal history and she needed to acknowledge his concerns. They talked and agreed to set up a separate account for "fun activities," to which each would contribute after all the bills and a pre-planned percentage for savings were taken care of. This satisfied Jeff's concern about savings and gave Cathy the incentive to discover ways to save a little extra in order to satisfy both of their goals.

The "balcony" approach gave Cathy a greater appreciation for Jeff's successes in life and for his commitment to their family. The"under-the-skin" approach let her understand that he wasn't saying no because he was mean-spirited and it wasn't because he didn't want to spend time with her alone. In fact, it was his love for her—as he perceived it—that had led to his no-saying.

As You Analyze Stressful Situations

Determine the best measures to take, consider the time-honored values that you uphold and make sure your proposed actions are those of a sincere, kind person who considers the needs of others as well as her own needs. After all, now and then, everyone needs to be reminded about what is really important in life.

Once you make a decision about how to respond, abide by it, acknowledging that the only behavior you can change is your own. Your attitude about this situation will automatically be reflected in your behavior. Be sure the attitude you display is the attitude you want to project. We can't change others' attitudes, but we can help someone see the value of change if we approach discussions creatively and constructively—not accusingly or destructively. And, remember, no one should get her way all the time. If you can't change something, don't sweat it and don't stress over it. Realize that you cannot control another adult's actions.

Amazing things can happen when we consciously change our attitude and act on the change. Many marriage counselors tell us that a positive change in attitude by both partners can turn a crumbling marriage around in a matter of weeks. That kind of result is definitely worth a try! Attitude change is a most powerful tool to include in our personal toolbox.

The Impact Your Personality Has on Others

"Everyone lives by selling something." Robert Louis Stevenson

We have all met people justifiably admired for their warmth, sincerity, and generosity. We also know people who are difficult to engage, distant, and unfriendly. If we're generous, we'll give those individuals an out by shrugging and saying, "That's just her. We've learned to ignore her difficult moods," or "She's the kind of person who needs to monopolize the conversation, so we just let her talk." But, unfortunately, difficult people don't understand the impact of their behavior and attitudes on others. They are, indeed, their own worst enemies.

According to scientists, our personalities are a mixture of genetics and individual experiences. We inherit a genetic predisposition, but the environment in which we are raised can modify our personality for better or worse. We need to understand our unique personality and our early experiences that helped forge it, and then we must train ourselves to become conscious of the ways our attitudes can help or hurt us and others.

We need to be aware of the verbal and non-verbal messages our attitudes send, often without our thought or intention.

Even brief negative situations are powerful and damaging. Take, for instance, an afternoon when a cranky teenager suddenly throws her books down and slams the door to her bedroom without explaining why. Or when a spouse comes home and speaks sharply to you and the children. Their attitudes have an immediate, negative, and even frightening impact on everyone else in the home. For good or ill, behavior can trigger a domino effect: one happy encounter with an encouraging friend can brighten up the gloomiest of days for you and you in turn pass on to others that encouragement.

Conversely, someone blaring a car horn at you or a boss singling you out for criticism in public can set a downward spiral into motion, and a good day suddenly becomes a terrible day—for you and for people around you.

And then there are those people who seem completely self-consumed. Pushy people and proverb writers know that "the crying baby gets fed first," "the squeaky wheel gets the grease," and "the early bird gets the worm." Persistence is important, but an overextension of persistence can backfire when the "pushed" person gets tired or obstinate and refuses to listen to what we have to say.

Understanding the impact of our personalities on the people around us is critical.

If we are oblivious, mean-spirited, a gossip, or uncaring about others' perspectives, we will severely limit our influence and someone else's chances for self-fulfillment. "Reading" different personality types and observing the person's facial expressions, body language, and posture can alert us to potential problems. If we can recognize problems before they become serious, we can adjust our personality tendencies and improve our communication methods.

That skill is necessary for everyone. If we have an idea or product to sell, we need to understand how our "customer" communicates and makes meaning. Literally and figuratively, we need to "speak" the same language.

Columbia Business School introduced a program that teaches the importance of acquiring a more empathetic and sensitive leadership style in business. Daniel Goleman, whose book "*Social Intelligence*" is part of the curriculum, points out, "While women are, in general, better at reading emotions, men tend to be better at managing them during a crisis. Women tend to be more sophisticated in reading social interactions, but also tend to ruminate more when things go wrong."

Neenu Sharma, a former MBA student in the Columbia program, says the moral of the story is this: "Leadership works best with both sexes involved. You may see the benefit of having the woman there to know what's actually going on, but you can also see the benefit of masculine traits when dealing with the critical emotions at the time."

As we discussed earlier, our perceived and predicted behavioral patterns correlate with our mindset, attitude, and personality. Science can help us understand that our body, mind, and spirit work together as we interact with others. If we want to be successful, personally as well as professionally, we need to make sure the three work together in harmony.

Neurobiology has proven that our brain detects patterns of behavior and imbeds them into our responses. We can certainly change our responses to stressors in our lives—but change requires commitment and conscious problem-solving techniques to break long-term negative patterns of behavior. We need to understand on a daily, hourly, even minute-by-minute basis that our attitudes are contagious. They impact others. We want to be aware of how we truly want them to impact others—and what the consequences are when we make those decisions.

Moving ahead...

Self-understanding is as important in the professional world as it is in our personal lives. As we mature, our responsibilities increase, we face bigger challenges, and we are exposed to a broader range of personalities and challenges. It isn't enough to be self-aware, we must also be "other-aware" if we want to relate harmoniously with the people around us. In the long run, self-knowledge will make the difference between success and mediocrity.

This does not mean that we should compromise our values in order to climb ladders. Quite the contrary. The more ably we maneuver through situations, the more we become confident in our abilities and the more we learn to appreciate individuals' differences. Appreciation and positive support are critical in every aspect of our lives. Every day small companies and divisions of Fortune 500 giants have to re-learn that lesson.

Management can make or break a company's image, profitability, and ability to attract and retain good people. Research has proven that employees leave organizations because of bad management, not because of the work involved. Bosses who are insensitive, overly critical, untrustworthy, distrustful, and micromanaging can destroy an organization. They fail to realize that employees are not fixed assets, they are free agents. And, if those free agents value their personal well being and recognize their need for self-fulfillment, they will move on rather than endure a negative work environment. Frequent turnovers are signs of a sick company and a potentially fatal management style.

The flip side of the coin is that bosses who frequently and sincerely express appreciation for excellent work and extra efforts will forge a cohesive and effective team. These are the bosses who look for opportunities to develop their people, who give credit where credit is due, and who inspire others to learn and do their best.

At some stage, successful people realize that they cannot change anyone but themselves, so they focus their energies on improving the ways they deal well with others. They become more aware of the impact of their default personality tendencies on others, and they polish the behaviors that are most helpful in successful communications.

Their secret to success?

They don't try to change who they are. Instead, they adapt to other personality types by understanding what the other person needs from them. We can all learn to manage our communication styles to meet the needs and expectations of others. When we help someone meet a need, that person will help us do the same.

Take a Personal Inventory

Understanding our strengths and abilities is the key to building and maintaining positive relationships. The only way to do this is to examine our limitations and know how to work around them in our dealings with others.

What is the best way to get to know ourselves better? We have already discussed a variety of personality types and the on-line resources that can reveal amazing things about our own unique approach to life. We need to take the time to identify just who we are. Assessments are eye-opening and they can be fun to take—after all, who do we find more fascinating than ourselves? By understanding our behavioral tendencies, we will gain the ability to adapt our behaviors to others in a constructive way. We all need to be aware of our personal hot buttons and how we can manage them.

We Get What We Tolerate

"Everyone's values are defined by what they will tolerate when it is done to others." William Greider

What negative behaviors do you tolerate in others?

When we look closely at relationships, we can be surprised at what we learn about ourselves. For instance, if we are allergic to smoke and yet never mention that fact to a friend who comes into our home and lights up a cigarette, what does that say about us? If we work best in an orderly, organized environment, yet we put up with a teenager's chronic disregard for the laundry basket, dishwasher, and our house rules, what does that say about us?

The message is this: We get the behavior that we tolerate.

When a doctor prescribes a new medication, we read and/or discuss its directions and list of side effects before we decide whether that medication will be effective for us. The same thought process should be applied both at work and at home. We should evaluate each situation, determine what side affects we can tolerate and which are unacceptable. Then there is another step: we must communicate our decisions, and follow up on them.

Do you remember the common cliché, the elephant in the room? It refers to a problem that everyone is well aware of, but the group has set up a conspiracy of silence because nobody is willing to deal with the issue.

We tell ourselves that we don't want to spill the apple cart but guess what, if we ignore the apples for too long, they'll rot. We consciously or subconsciously hope that if we ignore the problem, it will go away. And so we avoid taking any action—and sooner or later we learn that our failure to act early aggravates the problem.

If everyone in the office or at home knows what is going on and the situation is impossible to ignore, then why do we hide the problem under a rug, bury our head in the sand, or sit under a cone of silence? Perhaps, we just don't have the energy to take the required action. Perhaps, we're afraid to speak up, or we dislike confrontation and controversy. Perhaps, we worry that we'll be setting ourselves up for ridicule or embarrassment.

We are all tempted at one time or another to ignore upsetting aspects of our personal or work lives, hoping that they will disappear of their own accord (which, let's face it, very seldom happens). We might tell ourselves, "We just don't need the aggravation" or "Some things are better left unsaid." But remember the adage "No pain, no gain." Seeking painless solutions to life's tensions, repeating behaviors that have failed in the past, or taking the safe route for fear of a negative response does not improve the situation. Postponing action only means that the problem grows. Then, when action finally becomes unavoidable, we will find ourselves facing much greater challenges.

The elephant we are trying to ignore may be our alcohol abuse or someone else's, financial concerns that we fail to handle, an apology we should have made long ago, a discussion that needs to take place... the list is endless. We encourage you to reflect on whether your head is (figuratively speaking, of course!) buried in the sand. If you have been tolerating a certain behavior to avoid conflict, chances are good that what you have been tolerating has grown from a minor problem into a major problem.

When we fret about things that are not important, we waste precious energy and time. How much more time and energy are wasted and worried away when we fail to address the important concerns in our lives?

Avoidance can even be dangerous to our health if the situation is sufficiently stressful. We don't need to become overzealous in addressing every single little thing that bothers us—but we do need to recognize the difference between a minor issue that can be tolerated and a major issue that has the potential for headaches, heartaches, and problems in the future. We can let the former wash off our backs. We need to tackle the other problems before they spiral out of control.

Now, we don't need to be the bad cop or the intolerant parent. To paraphrase Aristotle, We should seek to address the issues that are important to us, at the right time, for the right reason, and in the right way.

Let's look at an example.

The Situation:

Your partner is working excessively long hours and missing dinner and bedtime with the children, even though he values family time. He explains that the economy is tough and it is important to be seen at work burning the midnight oil. As part of your value system, this situation needs to be addressed.

The Solution:

Wait for a non-stressful, quiet time where you can relax together and discuss the options. Look at all possible solutions together, then mutually decide on a course of action. Often serious problems may need "thinking time" after the discussion. But don't leave the situation hanging. Make a plan that will work for both of you, and agree to look at the results. If the plan becomes impractical or ineffective, agree to make another plan. Stick with the issue until it is solved.

In order to arrive at a win-win situation, we all need to determine which are minor irritants in life (things you can shrug off or grin and bear) and which are important stands you need to take.

Use the Art of the Question

Use reflective and information-seeking questions to better define the issue. Writing down a few short questions before discussing the situation should help you prepare. Allow the individual to articulate his or her view of the situation. Remember, every issue has at least two sides. You may learn something vitally important if you listen carefully to what is being said—and to what you believe is not being said. Work calmly and constructively towards an agreement that will outline how the two of you can best handle future challenges.

Reviewing the Sample Issue:

Your partner is working excessively long hours, missing meals and children's bedtime. This makes you feel overworked, underappreciated, and upset for the children's sake as well as your own.

Typical questioning techniques:

Tell me about the need for long hours.

Is there more than meets the eye?

Do we agree that family time is important?

Can we explore some options?

What would be helpful?

Is there anything that could be done differently?

Would making a plan help?

How will we follow up?

Write your own short questions that will open discussion for your own concerns:

Be Supportive

Remember: Think win-win! Use an unemotional, information-seeking, and conversational tone.

DO NOT ask a question whose answer you already know.

DO NOT allow yourself to whine, sound upset, or accuse.

Focus on the future rather than the past. Engineer a mutual commitment for what specific actions will be taken within an agreed-upon time.

Understand that the situation won't end with the conversation. You both need to encourage the other to arrive at a solution, and you need to show appreciation for the other's willingness to make a mutual commitment. Then schedule follow-ups on the plan's execution. Decide together whether the solution is working. If not, mutually agree to make adjustments. Remember: the success or failure of this process will depend upon communication, caring, and concern.

Some couples actually write up a contract with each other, signifying the seriousness with which they take their relationship, just as an agent and athlete do.

Choose what works for you, but remember that common courtesy goes a long way. Thank your husband, partner, child, colleague, boss, or friend for the opportunity to work together to clear the air and correct a situation that had gone awry.

Try journaling how you handled the situation, to learn from mistakes and celebrate successes—and then repeat them when necessary.

Self-Sabotage

"Until you value yourself, you will not value your time. Until you value your time, you will not do anything with it." M. Scott Peck

Looking from the outside in, it is easy to see how some people fall short of achieving their personal or professional goals. It is never as easy to be as perceptive with ourselves, however.

We all receive countless messages from family members, colleagues, and friends, and we consciously or subconsciously pick and choose which to incorporate into our minds. Often what we have been told and have come to believe does not align with our own experience or personal reality. We need to be aware of the power of those messages in our lives. Some messages can motivate us to do great things; others can destroy us. The question we want to ask ourselves is, "Why am I allowing the opinions of others to influence my behavior?"

Everyone has received messages that are not only untrue, but have the power to destroy our motivation and our sense of self. Examples might include, "That's a woman's job," "You're not very good at managing people. I am, so let me handle that," "You're destined to be overweight; it runs in the family," "You'll never amount to much," "Your ideas just won't work," "That's not what you should be doing," and on and on and on. It is dangerous to internalize these messages and convince ourselves that the speakers know us better than we know ourselves so we should believe them. Self-sabotage happens subtly and insidiously. It happens when we fail to address what is and is not true. Often fear or indecision causes us to accept rather than reject the messages. That was the case for Mark.

"You can't do that. Don't even try. I'll do it—after all, I'm an engineer." Mark is in his mid-50s now, but that message from his father continues to ring in his ears, deterring him from tackling many household projects that he is more than capable of addressing. In retrospect, he realizes that his father probably didn't appreciate the impact his directions had on him.

Fear definitely has a dark side. It distorts our thoughts. Most of us dread confrontations, so we live with a situation, feeling powerless to make a change—and that situation, therefore, continues to frustrate and upset us. Then our lives start to feel like a downhill slide. We begin to doubt ourselves and the intentions of others. We stay stuck in emotionally-charged situations, and our stress levels rise even higher.

When we fail to make our position crystal-clear, we position ourselves for misinterpretation and potential problems. We can't really blame others because we haven't clarified our own values, goals, and attitudes. Self-sabotage happens when we deny our responsibility to ourselves. We might ignore our own goals or personal limits because we are trying to please others. People then begin to change their expectations of us, mistakenly believing that we really want to get coffee for those attending our meeting or that we really don't mind working nights and weekends because we're single.

When we fail to correct those misperceptions, the damage is done. And the downward spiral begins.

Realize We Cannot Control Others

Although we cannot control the beliefs and opinions of others, we can control how we respond to them.

Ideally, as we mature, we learn to set limits successfully and define our personal boundaries. Many people will make demands or have expectations about our time, our talents, our energy, our money and our emotions.

It is up to you to choose what is appropriate for you. You should be the only person in the driver's seat of your own life. Every choice you make relates to time management, stress levels, and your ultimate satisfaction or unhappiness.

We all function like digital recorders, repeatedly playing the messages imbedded within our psyches, whether they are upbeat and happy or depressing and destructive. These messages begin in early childhood and continue to the present day, although we are particularly vulnerable in childhood, adolescence, and early adult years. One friend remembers her mother saying every day, "Think positive thoughts and positive things will happen" and "You are such a smart girl."

Those are positive messages that will reap great benefits. However, she also remembers other themes: "Women aren't good at making business decisions," "It's not ladylike to ask for something; wait and see if it's offered," "Beauty is as beauty does," and dozens of others.

She needed to sort through those internal messages that caused her to take certain actions—or, more often than not, caused her to fail to take action. We all need to do the same.

What are the "theme songs" playing in your internal iPod? What messages did you inherit from family members, teachers, friends, colleagues, and other authority figures?

Take the Negative Messages and Turn Them into Positives

We Need to Change Outdated Beliefs

"There is only one cause of unhappiness: the false beliefs you have in your head, beliefs so widespread, so commonly held, that it never occurs to you to question them." Anthony de Mello

There is no such person as "Superwoman." We need to change outdated beliefs that tell a woman it is her responsibility to do it all.

A belief system is the foundation upon which we build our lives. Beliefs are those ideas we assume to be true about the world, others, and ourselves. Our beliefs are inextricably linked to our behaviors and our expectations of others. Changing our beliefs requires changing our behavior, so it is important to be clear about our beliefs.

To quote Catherine Pratt in her book "Changing Core Beliefs," "Changing core beliefs can sound like a daunting task if it's a way of thinking you have had for a long time. But it isn't really." She emphasizes the point that we must become aware of exactly what lies within our belief system (ideas we inherited, adopted, or had imposed) before we can do anything about them.

The process starts by sitting down and making a list of all the things we believe in. Choose categories: religion, politics, family life, friendships, home life, work life, who I am. Identify the trash that needs throwing out. Put an X through those items on the list. Once we become aware of beliefs that are no longer relevant, we need to observe how we behave under those circumstances—and then we need to change our behaviors.

For example, if you believe that it is your responsibility to accomplish tasks that were traditionally allotted to women, such as laundry, then you will be acutely aware when the hamper overflows. If you have other, more pressing concerns, the laundry will add to your stress. Over time, these seemingly harmless and mundane beliefs will take an emotional toll on you, becoming increasingly burdensome. Emotions clue us into the time when we need to change unrealistic beliefs. If, for instance, we change the way we think about laundry obligations, then our behavior will change. New belief: Everyone dirties the clothes, so it is reasonable that everyone shares these duties.

Beliefs are power—both as motivations toward defining and grasping our goals and deterrents from dreaming and reaching them. If you believe that you will "never be in management" then your appearance, your attitude, your work style, and the relationships that you forge will reflect this point of view. The message here is to choose your belief system so it can do you and those you love the most good.

Should you want to be part of the management team, the first step is the most critical: you must believe that you will become management by both dressing and playing the part. Only then can you set to work to enact the belief. We can learn from those we admire, ask questions, keep our ears open for new opportunities, and volunteer to take on high profile projects, share cost-saving, or offer innovative ideas. In other words, actions are a result of our beliefs.

If at first you don't succeed, try, try again. Hold onto your positive belief and keep it first and foremost on your mind and, if necessary, change the course to your goal. Keep that positive can-do attitude.

To quote Tony Robbins, "All personal breakthroughs begin with a change in beliefs. So how do we change? The most effective way is to get your brain to associate massive pain to the old belief. You must feel deep in your gut that not only has this belief cost you pain in the past, but it's costing you in the present and, ultimately, can only bring you pain in the future. Then you must associate tremendous pleasure with the idea of adopting a new, empowering belief."

After Thought

"As long as a person doesn't know what (s)he doesn't know, (s)he doesn't grow." John Maxwell

Every team member, presumably, loves the game and the sense of working together toward a common goal of scoring some wins.

But one of the most important components of team building and development is the role of the coach. The coach offers insights into the game, plans for new ways of doing things, and is clear on the team's objectives on strategies.

Coaches are not only veterans of the game, they study it, analyze successes and failures, and guide the players to perform to their best. They inspire, motivate and ultimately want the best for the team and for each of their players.

The coaching role works as well in the business world as it does in the sports world. Because coaching is a confidential one-on-one relationship, it not only delivers results but is known to prevent problems. It integrates practical behavioral change over time by deepening an awareness of the individual's unique strengths as a foundation for improvement.

Participants benefit from the wisdom, knowledge and proven expertise of the coach.

What is Mentoring?

When one considers mentoring, the image of a seasoned corporate sage conversing with a young recruit comes to mind. Although there is a grain of truth in this statement, real mentoring is simply when someone helps another learn something that she would not learn if left alone. Mentors are trusted advisors who draw from their own personal experience to offer guidance. They usually will take a long, industry-wide view to help the individual navigate the business terrain.

Mentoring can occur naturally, informally or formally.

It can be a formal part of a program within a professional organization or an informal relationship.

It can last a day, several weeks, just long enough to help an individual over a "hump," or it can last several years. We usually encourage our clients to seek out several mentors over the course of their career.

Corporate sponsored mentoring is sometimes used to achieve strategic business goals, such as retaining new employees and/or for leadership succession planning.

A mentor could be a highly visible and experienced company executive advising a rising star. Although a senior manager may be helpful to your career, working with someone from outside your organization, who is not invested in organizational politics, can ensure that conversations, concerns, and issues are kept in strict confidence. An experienced executive/business coach will also offer an objective view from the outside looking in.

All career-minded individuals can benefit from a mentor.

To start, consider approaching at least two individuals you admire for their achievements. Ask if they would be willing to mentor you. Most successful people will be flattered. Everyone appreciates the chance to share their experience and knowledge—although they may or may not have available time. Don't be afraid to ask, all they can do is turn you down because of other commitments. On the other hand, should they agree, you should gain valuable insight.

Be sure to respect their time and confidentiality. And be prepared for your conversations. Arrive ready to discuss issues that are most important to you—don't waste your time with chitchat. Meeting with a mentor six times a year for approximately an hour or so would be appropriate.

You might also ask if impromptu phone calls would be welcomed. In this way, you can discuss important issues as they arise. It will be important that you, in some way, make the relationship reciprocal.

What is Coaching?

Unlike most mentors, a coach is less visible, but very much present.

We sometimes call ourselves invisible partners. Coaches are normally drawn from outside the organization, to provide individual—and, most importantly, confidential—support on personal, career and business matters.

Coaching is about partnering in a thought-provoking and creative process that inspires you to maximize your personal and professional potential.

The coaching relationship is a strong, resilient, dependable, and safe vehicle in which the need is identified and positive growth can take place. Professional coaches provide an ongoing partnership designed to help you produce fulfilling results and enhance the quality of your life. A coach is a listener, sounding board, and awareness-raiser.

Coaching creates a safe climate for purposeful dialogue. This is why it is important that the coach be from outside the organization.

Among other things, an Executive/Business Coach will help you learn to:

Develop your leadership abilities

Improve interpersonal skills

Move beyond self-imposed limitations

Align yourself with corporate objectives

Manage staff through increased personal effectiveness

Embrace feedback as an improvement tool

Bolster your self-determination

Understand the necessity of good communications

Key into gender-based behavior

Improve your decision-making skills

Develop your team-building know-how

Utilize proven conflict-resolution techniques

Take more than one perspective on issues

Understand the environment in which you work

Improve your problem-solving abilities

Develop a flexible management style

Plan an appropriate approach

Execute winning business strategies

Develop a talent pool and create loyalty

Cultivate a network that helps you and your organization

Establish priorities and receive exceptional performance reviews

Balance work and life priorities

Each of us has been given the gift of choice and the power to act. How we do that is up to us. Executive coaches routinely offer their clients a safe and confidential environment in which they can share both their personal and professional concerns.

Here is what one client said about her coaching experience: *"One of the most important business lessons that I learned came through my work with Executive Coach John Agno when I realized that I wasn't operating with internal integrity.*

It is important to know, understand, and accept all of yourself – idiosyncrasies and all. You are better at some things and worse at others. Know your strengths and blind spots. No one is perfect and no one fits in everywhere.

Be true to yourself and who you are. You are happiest when you are in alignment inside and out." Faith Fuqua-Purvis

Six in ten large North American corporations today recommend personal leadership coaching to their executive team. We hope you consider that as one of your personal development options.

About the Authors

Barbara A. McEwen is well known as a highly experienced executive, business owner, and seasoned master coach who works with senior executives to help them identify and assess personal development opportunities. Her unique, practical, and powerful strategies make her easy to talk to. She has a way of demystifying what it takes to become more effective. Her coaching deepens the clients' awareness of their unique strengths as a foundation for improvement.

Visit Barb's website at:
http://www.2020executivewomen.com

John G. Agno is a seasoned corporate executive, entrepreneur and management consultant who today coaches senior executives and business owners to reach decision-making clarity by exploring unintended consequences of their future actions.

John helps you see things you are missing, affirms whatever progress you have made, tests your perceptions and lets you know how you are doing. His developmental coaching helps you focus your natural abilities in the right direction.

The coaching allows your inner-potential to erupt upward through effective leadership; to develop commitment within organizations and in a world of "free agents" and "volunteer" talent.

Visit John's websites and blogs for more specific information:

www.CoachedtoSuccess.com

www.SelfAssessmentCenter.com

www.ExecutiveCoaching.us.com

www.CareerWomenCoaching.com

www.BusinessCoaching.us.com

www.LifeSignature.com

www.CoachingTip.com

www.SoBabyBoomer.com

www.Ask-Know-Do.com

For free leadership tips by Coach Agno via email, click here to subscribe or sign up at: www.WhatisLeadership.info.

Other Books by the Authors:

"**_When Doing It All Won't Do:_ _A self-coaching guide for career women_**" by Barbara McEwen & John G. Agno

Purchase at **Amazon for the Kindle Edition**

Women
and
Time

John G. Agno + Barbara A. McEwen

Women and Time

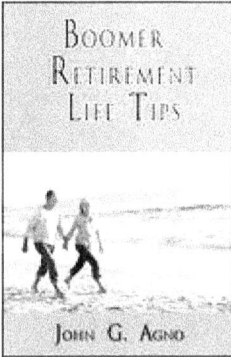

Boomer Retirement Life Tips explores their personal strategy and saving for retirement to where they will retire, how to handle aging parents and adult children, to health and wellness tips for aging like fine wine and deciding on a phased retirement or encore career.

Sample or purchase Kindle Edition

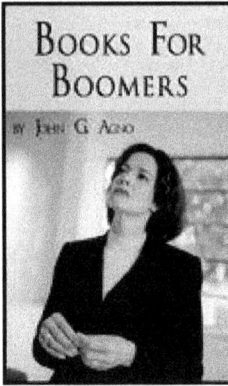

With the oldest boomers reaching 65 years of age in 2011, this book explores a wide range of issues: <u>love</u>, marriage, friendship, hopes, happiness, <u>encore careers</u>, <u>health</u>, <u>fitness</u>, parenting and <u>aging</u> along with <u>retirement readiness</u>.

<u>Books for Boomers: Reviews & Coaching Tips</u>

<u>Back to Table of Contents</u>

Kindle Edition (preview or buy): Can't Get Enough Leadership: Book Notes & Coaching Tips

Looking for a unique gift idea? When you give a Coached to Success gift certificate, you will be remembered every day of the year. Subscribe to daily ...or... weekly leadership tips from world-class teachers at **www.CoachedtoSuccess.info**

Back to Table of Contents

www.ingramcontent.com/pod-product-compliance
Lightning Source LLC
Chambersburg PA
CBHW071821020426
42331CB00007B/1577